EBURY PRESS
THANK YOU FOR LEAVING

Rithvik Singh is the bestselling author of *I Don't Love You Anymore* and *Warmth*. With a degree in English literature from Hansraj College, University of Delhi, and an unceasing love for writing, he writes to give hope to those looking for it. Formerly a content lead at a storytelling company, Rithvik left his corporate job in 2024 to be a full-time author. With over 5,00,000 followers on Instagram (@wordsofrithvik), his words never fail to feel like home to his readers. Several celebrities have shared his words, including Britney Spears and Huda Kattan, and he has been invited as a speaker to several prestigious institutions across India. Rithvik won the Atta Galatta-Bangalore Literature Festival Book Prize (popular choice) for *I Don't Love You Anymore* in 2024. He lives with his family in Udaipur, but his heart belongs to Delhi. On days when he's missing deadlines, he can be seen struggling (snuggling) with his cat, Cameron, who finds his laptop cosier than any place in the world for a nap.

thank you
you
for
leaving

learning to be okay
with saying goodbye

RITHVIK
SINGH

EBURY
PRESS

An imprint of Penguin Random House

EBURY PRESS

Ebury Press is an imprint of the Penguin Random House group of
companies whose addresses can be found at global.penguinrandomhouse.com

Published by Penguin Random House India Pvt. Ltd
4th Floor, Capital Tower 1, MG Road,
Gurugram 122 002, Haryana, India

First published in Ebury Press by Penguin Random House India 2025

ISBN 9780143474661

Typeset in Adobe Garamond Pro by MAP Systems, Bengaluru, India
Printed at Thomson Press India Ltd, New Delhi

www.penguin.co.in

For my mother,
thank you for staying

This book is an ocean full of feelings, so if, at any point, you feel like you're drowning, keep the book down for a moment and remind yourself that it's a privilege to feel emotions as intensely as you do. Because some people are so disconnected from their hearts that they don't allow themselves to feel anything at all.

That being said, I'm sorry, but I'm going to break your heart all over again and also fix it at the same time.

I wish you a happy reading.
This book will make you cry.

The more love I give you,
the emptier I feel.
I think I'll only be okay again
when I ask you to leave.

The older I get, the more I understand why poets are so obsessed with rain. I feel sad for the people who shut their windows when it rains instead of stepping out and letting the raindrops make love to their souls. I hate the idea of umbrellas and raincoats. Why would you want to protect yourself from something that intends to heal your heart? Why would you choose to run away from the rain when you can dance in it?

I think you can tell a lot about how much pain someone is in by how much they claim to hate the rain.

So many of us want to dance in the rain but stop ourselves from doing it. Every time it rains, we find the people around us running for shelter. When it rains, let your heart be a paper boat and allow it to be drenched completely. Let your hair be caressed by raindrops and your skin be kissed. Dance your heart out in the rain to heal your heart. There are so many people who are so used to hiding their hearts that they no longer feel the urge to make love to the rain. Don't lose yourself like them. *The rain has its own magical ways of making your heart feel lighter.*

We hurt each other so much that when we finally decided to talk about things, we couldn't say anything.

I remember us sitting near the library, under a tree, trying to understand why we hurt each other so much. Cars came and went. The traffic was loud, but the silence between us was deafening. I knew you were hurt. You knew you were hurting me. We both knew our fights weren't normal. We knew two people who truly loved each other wouldn't treat each other that way. There was a time when we would break ties with anyone who would want us to stay apart. Who knew we'd end up breaking each other's hearts?

If you love someone, show them kindness, even in moments of conflicts and arguments. Some things you might say can cause damage that no amount of love can fix. The next thing you know, wounds take the place of love. Hurtful words grow like wildflowers in your veins. They become a part of you. You know you love that person, and they know they love you. Yet, because of the hurtful things said in the heat of the moment, you both start to believe you deserve better.

Don't let a wonderful love story turn into a tragedy because you let your anger take over you.

When someone tries to erase their name from your soul, they end up erasing a lot more.

The way you can't listen to that one song anymore. The way you look away every time you cross that one restaurant. Watching the sunset together isn't the ideal date idea for you anymore. You're no longer excited about your birthday. You don't expect handwritten letters. You no longer overthink when someone doesn't respond to your text for hours. You say goodbye without tears in your eyes. You don't feel like going the extra mile. You dislike the chocolate you once loved. You went to the mountains with them all the time and now force yourself to be a beach person.

What nobody tells you about love is that when someone you love leaves, you end up closing the door on a lot of other things you love too.

The one whose name comes to you while you're driving a car, doing your laundry, talking to a friend, meeting someone new after a long time, visiting a familiar cafe, reading a sad book, listening to a song you were once hooked on, sitting alone on a park bench or while sitting with someone on a park bench—that's the person you cannot be with anymore. That's the person you've loved the most. That's the person who left. You don't need a reason to remember them. It's their memories your blood is composed of.

Here's what loving someone who doesn't love you back feels like:

When you're watering a plant for weeks and a few days before your eyes can see flowers, your little pet visits you, plucks the roots out and destroys it unknowingly. He thinks it's a game.

It's raining, and you decide to share your umbrella with someone. They don't thank you for it and also take the umbrella with them, holding someone else's hand. You're still there, drenched in something that was never meant to even touch you.

A bridge where two lovers are holding hands and kissing each other. You run towards it, hoping to find your soulmate somewhere around, but the bridge collapses. The lovers die in front of your eyes.

An airport where you hear so many goodbyes, it makes you claustrophobic. You watch so many people break into tears that you end up breaking too.

You would bring flowers from the garden every day and put them in the vase on the dining table. The room smelt of roses, but my heart smelt of emptiness. You never brought flowers for me. You're in a different city now, and I wish you knew the flowers in the vase aren't the only thing dying in your absence.

I've been trying to stitch my heart back together with the threads of your kindness and love, but the minute I remember that person, my heart falls apart all over again.

Imagine this—a farmer stands in the middle of a field, elated to see the harvest. He looks towards the sky to thank God, but raindrops fall on his face. A few at first, then a few more. Until he realizes, it's raining heavily, and all his crops are getting destroyed. This is what happens to me when I think of that one person. I've been stitching my heart back together, only for it to fall apart all over again. Hope is a bird with chipped wings. It doesn't fly in the garden of my life anymore.

You love me, and I know you're worthy of all my love and more, but how do I tell you that there's more trauma in me than blood? That no amount of love from your end can fix the damage that person did to me? I keep telling you that there's a fire in every room of my heart, and you tell me it will keep us both warm. You love me so much. I hate that I don't love you as much as you do. I hate that my tragedy is being constantly engulfed by the thoughts of someone who only ever gave me pain.

I start fires within me every night, hoping your memories will burn down once and for all. I still wake up to flowers that smell like you. I still wake up knowing even fire loves you so much, it gives warmth to your memories instead of burning them.

Love isn't a language
taught at schools,
and the tragedy
is that it isn't spoken
in homes either.

Love is a sparrow
in a room full of fans,
too scared to fly,
destined to die.

Love is a moral science
textbook in high school,
you'd rather do arithmetic
than listen to your soul.

Love is an English province
in colonial India,
caged in places
where it was meant to fly.

Love is a dead flower
lying on the street,
you step on it often
but never hear it weep.

Love is a sunflower
that cannot find the sun,
a railway station
that reeks of goodbyes,
a dandelion that
doesn't keep promises.

I'm convinced,
love is a sad gardener
with lilies in his hair
wrinkling alone in a world
that hates romance.

Children who grow up with angry fathers don't inherit the anger. They inherit silences so loud from their mothers that even storms feel like music to them. They grow up longing for love while also being perpetually scared of it. They fall in love with people who break their hearts because they cannot understand the kind of love that doesn't leave someone in pieces.

After a long, sunny day, you return home and dip your legs in water. You re-read your favourite book and surprisingly find new sentences to highlight. You find a shirt you love in your closet, one you thought was lost forever. You come across an old test paper from school with a 10/10 and a star given by the teacher. You take a shower, and the water is just the right temperature. You find an old handwritten note in the pocket of your jeans. You make coffee, and it tastes like heaven. You didn't change the recipe; it just happened. *The point is that you deserve someone who makes you feel exactly the way such moments do.*

Every time I visit my grandmother, my dearest *naani,*[*] I can't help but notice how she's losing weight. She's more wrinkled than before every time I see her. When she was young, her hair would trail below her waist—long, thick and lustrous at all times. Her hair is now a braid thinner than a line of ants. When we were kids, we would go to the park with her every day. She'd take a walk, and we'd play with the other kids. She can barely walk for a few minutes now and gets tired easily. A few years ago, she met with an accident. I went to visit her and the first thing she told me was, '*There's curry in the kitchen. Your favourite!*' There's nothing in the world that I cherish more than her. I could see that she was in pain. Her legs were plastered. But all she cared about was the curry in the kitchen her grandson would love. I don't know how big a heart it takes for this kind of love. I don't think most of us are capable of it. Every time I visit her, I try to spend a lot of time sleeping in her lap as she runs her fingers through my hair. It is as if by spending more time with her, I'll be able to preserve this feeling forever.

[*] Maternal grandmother.

Autumn is my favourite season. I have a thing for sad things—seasons, memories and people. When the earth is covered in gold, we get to see nature having a hard time letting go. Nature and I have this in common. When I have to say goodbye to someone, my entire body trembles, and my heart feels unsafe. Have you ever had chai in an earthen cup? Try tasting it once it has gotten cold. That's what goodbyes taste like. Hopeless romantics are made for kisses in the rain, ice creams on sunny days, matching anklets and handmade bracelets, sunsets that look like the backdrop of ancient paintings, and flowers that carry memories even after they have died and lost their fragrance. *Hopeless romantics are hopeless when it comes to saying goodbye.*

I'm so used to holding your hand while walking on the street that even when you're not with me, it takes me a while to make peace with how empty my hands and heart feel without you.

Whenever we meet, I start telling you my endless stories immediately, but the first thing you say to me is, '*Give me your hand.*' I give you my hand and you don't just hold it; you hold it in a way that makes every ounce of my soul feel loved. You don't just hold *my* hand. You hold the hand of the fifteen-year-old version of me who thought he didn't deserve to be loved. You hold the hand of the eighteen-year-old version of me who was heartbroken to the extent that he read every book on self-love and thousands of quotes on the internet only to realize that he hates himself regardless. You hold my hand, and my inner child forgets everything he has been through. *You hold my hand, and my heart comes back to me.*

Our mothers have spent a lifetime being kind to the people who were never kind to them. We've learned from their kindness when to stop being kind.

You ask me why I love sunsets, and I tell you that the way sunflowers are attracted to beginnings, I'm attracted to endings. And there's a certain comfort in knowing that endings aren't always scary. *When you leave, the setting sun will still be there to hold me.*

YOU
ARE
NOT
ALONE

You wake up in the middle of the night and open the fridge but do not find the aamras your mom used to make for you. You receive a call right at that moment. It's her. You realize you're miles away from each other, but she carries pieces of your soul in her *pallu*.[†] She doesn't like mangoes anymore. They taste like regrets in your absence. She regrets letting you go. She regrets choosing your dreams over proximity, but the regret is fleeting. She calls you and is instantly reminded that you're not *that* far after all. You're always around even when you're not. One day, you'll go back home—she'll make your favourite aamras for you, and it'll taste like heaven. '*I forgot to add sugar,*' she'll tell you. But you wouldn't realize it because it would have so much of her heart.

[†] The tail end of a dupatta.

Does the ocean also weep
on new moon days,
when the moonlight refuses to kiss it,
or is it just something poets do?

Grief stays on paper
instead of love these days.
My letters are no longer
an ode to your beautiful face.

There was a time when you'd
take tragedies in your arms
and turn them into poems.

Today, you're the tragedy
I'm trying to forget.
You're the pain,
you're the poem.

'How do I get over that person?' I asked the rain.

The rain replied, 'I've been trying to get over flowers for centuries but in vain. I once fought with the earth, but I fell for it again anyway.'

Some feelings are so deeply engraved on your heart that it doesn't matter how hard you try—whenever you see that person's face, your heart will turn into a raindrop. You won't be able to help but fall for them all over again.

If sunsets were oranges,
I'd peel and serve them
on a platter for you.

And if you ever
fell in love with me,
I'd do the same
with my heart too.

Why can't you stop fidgeting your legs? Why do your eyes carry sunsets and not sunflowers? What's hurting your heart? Let me rephrase that—*who* is hurting your heart?

You deserve smiles purer than the water from inaccessible streams in the mountains. You deserve someone who makes you happy to the point where you start trusting life again. You deserve someone who carries the colours of your favourite flowers in their heart and honesty in their eyes. You deserve someone who chooses to love you so deeply that the heaviness you're carrying within is left with no choice but to perish.

Love is what makes you sleep peacefully even when storms are raging outside, and trust me, your soulmate won't unleash storms within your soul.

Nobody teaches you
how to deal with
the atrocious ache
of losing love
for someone
whose name
was once synonymous
with love for you.

Dear heart,
why are you
falling out of love
with someone
who once made
all your dreams
come true?

I could feel
the knots in my heart
untangle after years
of hurting me,
the moment a knot tied
my heart to yours.

Don't tell me that you understand me
when your heart is a full moon night
and mine is a polluted sky,
too hazy for the stars to shine.

When you tell someone you love them, they only have a few seconds to respond. You're standing in front of them with your heart on a platter. Your feelings are the roses that adorn your heart. Anxiety grabs you by the throat and takes over your entire being. The sheer fear of being told that your feelings are yours alone makes your heart beat louder than ever. Every second spent with you was like those few seconds. The kind of anxiety I should've felt only while telling you that I loved you, I felt all the time. People tell you that they love you but always make you feel otherwise. *Insecurities spread like a forest fire inside you when the person you love is inconsistent with their love.*

You would bring me flowers after every fight.

You don't deserve to be loved.
I got you flowers.

If I didn't choose to date you, nobody else ever would.
I got you flowers.

I should've never broken up with my ex.
I got you flowers.

I'd happily forgive you, but flowers aren't bandages that fix the wounds caused by the thorns of careless words. My feelings for you are wildflowers that have taken over my heart. I'm learning to pluck them out from my heart so that one day, I can give you flowers too.

If your heart were a lily, I'd bury mine into the earth to be your home.

If your heart were an ocean, I'd be the river that always finds its way to you.

If your heart were a storm, I'd happily sacrifice my calm at the altar of love.

If your heart were grief, I'd trade happiness for it.

If your heart were a bird, I'd give you the entire sky.

If your heart were mine, I'd be the happiest person in the world.

Have you seen that one monument standing tall in the middle of a war? It's damaged but not entirely destroyed. It's surrounded by broken pieces of everything that once used to be around it. My heart and that monument have so much in common. My heart is burning in the aftermath of the love you failed to give me.

I've been trying to grow flowers in places where you left voids. Today, I saw you with someone else. I can feel the roses burning within me, carpeting every inch of my soul. How can seeing someone with another person make someone else feel so terribly alone?

I'd be lying
if I told you
that music runs
through my veins
every time your
eyes meet mine,
because your presence
does so much
more to me than
music can ever describe.

My heart is a flower,
and my blood, nectar,
and the butterflies
you give me
keep swirling
around it.

My soul is a story
translated too many times
by people who
couldn't understand
its original form.

The story's essence
is a wilted flower
on a busy street.
It reeks of filthy shoes
and cigarettes now.

Nobody remembers
it anymore.

Soothing sunsets
spent savouring
some soulful stories.

When you fell sick as a kid, your mom wouldn't sleep the entire night. You would even catch her secretly crying. As an adult, living away from home, you find yourself standing alone in your kitchen at 1 a.m., trying to find a medicine that would make your fever disappear. Your roommate is asleep and you don't want to wake them up. You want to call your mom but realize that while it will give you peace, it'll give her anxiety.

You realize you can hang out with people all day long only to stand in the middle of your kitchen at night all alone, trying to find medicines. You haven't had dinner, but nobody cares. You haven't slept properly in days, but nobody has noticed. You've been perpetually anxious, but nobody has been able to dissect the sadness in your eyes. You go to the doctor's clinic alone for the first time and a tear drops from your eyes. This is your rendezvous with loneliness.

You're away from home, constantly trying to feel at home. You realize there are people who love you, but nobody in the world loves you to the point where your illness makes their heart heavy. Nobody feels sick in the gut and has tears in their eyes when you're unwell. You wonder if it's even possible to find someone like that—someone who is terrified of seeing you in pain.

You check your phone and realize you have ten missed calls from Mom, your *home*. You call back, and she picks up and says, *'Is everything okay? I had a bad dream last night.'* You respond by saying, *'Yes, Mom, I'm all right'.*

It's funny how adulting makes you yearn for things you kept taking for granted all your life.

Growing up isn't about toys, stars and rainbows, when darkness feels more familiar than light, and fate never stops playing with your existence. What nobody tells you is that when you grow up with mountains growing on your chest, sometimes there's no room left for memories. When life constantly lets you down, you eventually learn not to let your hopes go up.

We still live in the same city, but it's not the same without *us*. Every time it rains, I close the windows, turn off the lights and bury my head in a pillow. I still remember dancing in the rain with you. Together, we were a poem that didn't care about how others interpreted it. Together, we knew we were art, no matter who could fathom our beauty and who couldn't. Have you found another person to dance with, in the rain? Does the song of their soul sound similar to mine?

Clingy friends are worth dying for.

The ones who want to include you in every party they're invited to. The ones who want you to be happy but also get a little jealous every time you talk about your new friends. The ones who take offence when someone says something even slightly bad about you. The ones you can call without dropping a text first and asking if it's okay to call at the moment. The ones who know your favourite movie isn't the one you ask everyone to watch—it's the one you never mention to anyone because you don't want to share it with others. The ones who know you feel too much. The ones who reassure you that just because you feel a lot doesn't mean *you* are a lot. The ones who love you the way the rain loves flowers and poets love stars. The ones who are there for you on days when your heart is breaking, and also on the days when it's blooming better than all your favourite flowers. There are some friends who make you feel like you've already found the loves of your life—hold on to them, always.

Things that instantly make me think, *I love this person so much:*

My best friend gets me flowers every time we meet. Sometimes it's a rose, sometimes a whole bouquet and when there's no flower shop around, it's a lily from a nearby garden. I do the same for her.

In college, my classes ended at 4 p.m., and my friend's ended at 1 p.m. He'd wait three hours only to hang out with me.

I received a text the other day that said, '*I know we've not been able to talk much lately, but I want you to know that I love you and I'm here for you. I'll call you in a bit, and I hope you know what an amazing person you are.*'

When things got extremely toxic between me and my ex, my friends made sure I didn't reach out to my ex. They would go out with me, arrange sleepovers with me and travel with me to my favourite places to keep me distracted.

A friend of mine went to Paris for the first time, and the moment they reached the Eiffel Tower, they called me and said, '*This would have been way more beautiful if you were here.*'

I'm convinced there's more beauty in friendship than most romantic relationships.

Let's build a relationship where we don't break each other's hearts during fights.

Where arguments are always less important than the love we have for each other. Where none of us wait for the other person to resolve a fight. Where the competition isn't about who wins the argument but who sorts it out first. Where our kids don't grow up hearing us fight at the top of our lungs. Where our home doesn't smell like violence but love. Let's build a relationship where our kids are fluent in the language of love and averse to aggression. A home made of people whose love for one another is a flower unbothered by storms and forest fires.

A store that sells
silk sarees,
a mother that waits
for the day
her daughter would
buy her one.

A father buys
ice cream for his kids,
but none for himself.
He loves ice cream.

I'm convinced
there's no love
in saying *I love you.*
Love is in
silk sarees,
ice cream by the lake,
parathas‡ made with extra ghee,
hand-knitted shirts,
tiny flowers
and freshly cut fruits.

---

‡ Layered flatbread.

There are people who are so kind to you that you can't help but wonder how they manage to carry so much light within themselves. Do they carry sunflowers in place of a heart? Have they soaked in all the light in the world and are now pouring it into every heart they touch? A few moments with them, and your heart feels lighter. A few more moments with them, and you crave a lifetime. Their kindness makes them more desirable than anyone you've ever met.

Every fall is a chance,
an opportunity to rise,
they told me,
but how do I tell them,
ever since I fell for you,
my soul has forgotten
how to fly and
my roots have spread
deep into the ground.
My wings are the manure
nourishing my roots—
they once helped me fly.

They told me
that in love,
we finally fathom liberation,
but I'm in love with someone
who cannot fathom my heart.

My existence is a boiling cauldron,
the scent of my burning heart
embraces everything in sight.
Funny how everything's gone,
but my love for you
keeps growing with
each passing night.

Look what your brutally tender touch has done to this heart—
it breathes within me but no longer belongs to me.

Feelings are like water
running through your heart.

You're drenched
and they don't even notice.

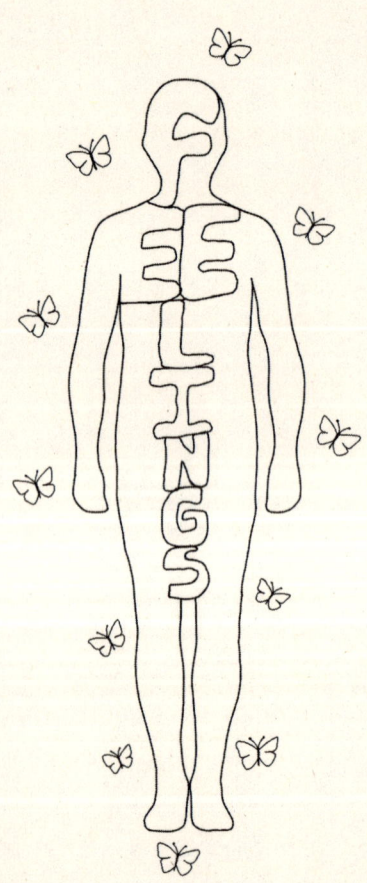

It's been quite a journey,
placing my heart everywhere
except where it belongs,
loving others in oceans
while forgetting
to calm my own soul.

The art of saying goodbye
without turning into a river
that somehow always
finds its way back
to the ocean
called their heart.

Your heart is not a jigsaw puzzle. There aren't pieces of you in other people. Finding someone who is completely in love with you won't complete you. They love you because you're art, not because they're the last piece to the puzzle called your heart. You're not a puzzle but a painting—and a beautiful one indeed—filled with colours and life—gorgeous at all times, with or without someone.

One day, you won't miss her.

All right, but how are you so sure about it? Do sunsets have an expiration date? Does the ocean get rid of water over time? Do flowers eventually start hating the colour of their petals? Do birds grow to loathe their wings?

In love, your soul turn into a beautiful design on the quilt called life. Your heart becomes a studio that only has room for music. Love doesn't come with an expiration date. Just because someone stopped loving you, it doesn't mean you'll stop loving them too.

People don't love and leave,
they love and keep loving
or they leave but stay—
sometimes, there are things
that remind you of them
every single day.

People who aren't a part
of your story anymore still manage
to remain a part of your stories.
How their smile
could melt hearts
and turn rivers into lakes,
for rivers won't have an option
but to stay still to see
their shimmering smile.

They smelt like jasmines
and rose garlands
kept outside temples;
their beauty butchering
the atheist in you.

What they don't
teach you at school
is that there are people
you will meet,
and they will teach you
what love really means,
but eventually,
even they will leave.

There are some people
who are so beautiful,
they're the morning sun personified;
and whether they love you
or feel nothing for you,
meeting them changes
your whole life.

There's an ending more gorgeous than sunsets—it's when, at the end of the day, you lie next to me, and I watch you slowly fall asleep while reading a book. I'm convinced your eyelashes were curled personally by God. I'm convinced my sunsets are prettier than the rest of the world's.

With you,
the only language I speak
is that of the soul.
Syllables don't matter;
only sentiments do,
when someone
becomes your home.

You see them and turn into a flower being kissed by the sun for the first time. You're not used to this feeling, but you know they will make your heart bloom. You know you will cherish this feeling for a lifetime.

You know you're being loved the right way when your compassion grows, the empty spaces in your heart are filled with flowers and you do not wake up with headaches but have peaceful nights full of dreams. You can feel your heart melting as the trauma that hardened it reduces to dust. You can no longer remember the mountains you were carrying on your back because all you can see are the flowers you're carrying in your hands—the flowers they gave you. *You know you're being loved the right way when life doesn't seem all wrong anymore.*

There are people who will love you so much that they will miss you more than you would expect them to. They'll be at a cafe, see a painting and text you, '*I wish you were here. This painting immediately made me think about you.*' They'll find you more picturesque than all the paintings in the world. They'll be hanging out with their friends and still be thinking about you, giggling at an old joke you had cracked. Giggling at the fact that you can barely keep your eyes open when you're laughing your heart out. They'll understand you so well that they'll know when you're faking a smile in photographs. Their eyes will widen and their cheeks will turn pink when they think or talk about you. When someone mentions your name, they will feel almost as if someone has called them. If they could, they would gift-wrap their heart, place it inside your favourite book and gift it to you.

There are people who will love you so much that they will make scrapbooks full of your photographs, leave cute little notes of reassurance for you, and take polaroids of you to hang with fairy lights in their room. They will gift you little things (like a small bracelet) you can wear every day that make you think about them whenever you wear them, watch your favourite movie again and again so that they can talk about it to you, and create a playlist for you so that their most beloved songs can become yours too. They will travel for hours to meet you. They will be terrified to see you in pain. They will love you with their whole heart, secretly hoping that someday, you'd lend them space in your heart too. They will look at the sky coloured in crimson and flamingo pink and the only thing it will remind them of is the colour of your skin and how your beauty can make even the sunset sky jealous. Wait for that person.

Healing seems like a distant dream, and I would like to believe that I'm friends with my pain now. Is that why I keep coming back to you? Why do you never come back to me? My heart has a weird way of looking for happiness in the wrong places. I know you've hurt me over and over again, but I know I'm very much capable of falling in love with you again. I'm lying. I never fell out of love in the first place.

We all continue to carry
tenderness within us,
for someone who stole
the softness of our souls.

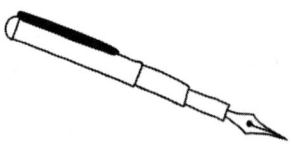

We're ink pens
in forgotten drawers,
flowers pressed inside books
yellowing in dusty libraries.

And they're
fresh journals that smell like summer,
books straight out of the press,
everything youthful,
everything unscathed by love.

There's an eighteen-year-old boy
who is convinced he doesn't
deserve to be loved,
that he doesn't have the kind of smile
that girls drool over,
but the kind of smile
people call *cute*.
He spends a lifetime
not smiling in photographs.

There's an eighteen-year-old boy
who is convinced he doesn't
deserve to be loved
because someone he loved
told him he's best-friend material
and not boyfriend material.
He's sensible, sensitive and smart
but he isn't the kind of boy
who gives you butterflies
when you watch him playing
on the basketball field.
He doesn't want to be anyone's
'best friend' anymore.

There's an eighteen-year-old boy
who is convinced he doesn't
deserve to be loved
because girls love spending time with him,
but they make sure nobody thinks
they're dating.

He's just a friend. I'm single.
He's just a friend. I'm single.
He's just a friend. I'm single.

There's an eighteen-year-old boy
who reads self-love quotes
on the internet but realizes self-love
isn't possible when nobody
has ever made him feel worthy of love.

There's an eighteen-year-old boy
who is the nicest person I know.
I wish people weren't *just nice* to him.

Waking up without you feels, for lack of a better word, pathetic. Your sun-lit smile is what used to add 'good' to all my mornings, but we were no good together. I know you don't even think about me anymore, but my thoughts are a temple where all the prayers are only about you. Soulmates were what we wanted to be, but we had no control over what we ended up becoming— two people who loved each other so much but just couldn't treat each other the right way. There's so much love left inside my heart for you, but my heart is in too many pieces for me to even consider getting back together with you.

My heart is a flower
my mother watered for years—
protecting it from storms,
forest fires,
placing her hands on it
when people tried to
step on it;
the wrinkles on her hands
are a testament to the same.

My heart is a flower,
my mother, the roots
that I forget to honour
on most days.
For when you're blooming,
you tend to forget
who made you bloom.

Thank you, mom,
for making flowers
bloom in a chest,
where my father
only ever wanted
to plant grief;
the same kind
he planted
in your soul.

When I was in school, I was the only kid in the class who was interested in reading. The only boy who didn't know how to play cricket. The academically brilliant kid who could never be cool enough to make friends. I always felt replaceable. The friend people hung out with when everyone else wouldn't pick up the call. The guy you would talk to when you needed help with studies. The guy you could vent to anytime, but who wouldn't ever vent to you. The guy who won't ever be invited to any parties but would help you pick an outfit every time. The good guy. The nice guy. The kind of guy who was nobody's favourite person. Because there was always someone cooler to hang out with. Always.

If you're someone who doesn't fit in, this is for you. You're not the problem. You just haven't found your soulmates yet. The kind of friends who wouldn't judge you for not knowing how to play cricket but hold your hand and teach you without making you feel bad about yourself. The kind of friends who would skip parties if you aren't invited as well because they believe it cannot be a party without you. The kind of friends who would seek your help while offering you endless love and care without you having to ask. The kind of friends who would ask if you're okay and if it's okay to vent to you at the moment.

You'll come across two kinds of people in life—the ones who will judge you for being different and the ones who will love you for it. Wait for the latter.

The last person
who broke my heart
told me that my heart
had no room for love.
I wanted to tell them,
*'I've finally made room
for love for myself
and that's what's
unsettling for you.'*

They told me that
my eyes had
the kind of sadness
no sunrise could take away—
that if I wished for the sun
of our relationship to set,
my whole life would be spent
searching for the light.

Light.
Light.
Light.
That's all that was ever there
before you came,
but you swallowed the moon
that sang songs to my soul,
replaced it with a thousand shooting stars
dying in front of my eyes
one after the other,
refusing to fulfil any of my wishes.

Sometimes I think
if I fell in love again,
they will find
more loneliness in me
than heart,
more sadness in me
than on a news channel,
a hundred daggers
plunged into a heart
that continues to bleed
but refuses to die.

Maybe if you take a shower, have a cup of tea, talk to a friend or go out, things won't get any better, and your heart won't feel lighter. But there's no reason to let your heart be an airplane stuck in turbulence when it can very much be at peace. It's a conscious choice you must make every morning as the sun kisses you—wanting and trying to get over someone until you finally do.

The problem is that
they'll ask you to
join the best business schools
and get the *best* jobs in the world
but abandon you
the moment you decide
to do what's
best for your heart.

The heart won't be valued
in rooms devoid of paintings—
homes so full of pragmatism
that they suffocate everyone living in them.

You were five
when your father told everyone
you'll become a doctor,
because he didn't know
art saves hearts too.

You were sixteen
when you realized
you cared more about Keats
than kinematics,
that you would rather spend
the entire day in the library
than a minute in the physics lab.
You said that to your father
and he laughed at you;
you never knew someone's
laughter could slaughter your heart
until it did.

71

The heart won't be valued
in rooms devoid of paintings,
and art can't be valued
by those who've lost their souls
to capitalism.

I know it's not that big a deal. It's just a text message. Maybe they did not get the time to respond to me. But my anxiety doesn't understand that.

They're breaking up with you.
Something terrible must've happened to them.
Who wants to talk to you anyway?
Told you, you're just a convenient option for them.
You thought someone could love you?

If this is what your anxiety tells you, listen to me. You'll find someone who will understand how significant something as seemingly insignificant as a text message is for you. Someone who will be surrounded by people and flooded by work but still choose to respond to you first. They'll look at their notifications and smile seeing your name. People will tease them with your name and tell them to stop being on their phone all the time. But they won't listen to them because they'd rather listen to your heart. You deserve someone who does not leave you questioning if you matter. Someone who ensures you feel loved, even when they're not around.

Your dark circles are poems
hanging under your eyes.
If I see silent stories
shimmering in your soul,
I shouldn't be surprised.

I know some of them
would leave me paralysed,
but please let me
read them all
before we say goodbye.

I kept trying to bring us on the same page, only to realize we were not even in the same book. We exist in two different sections in an old library. I'm poetry, and you, non-fiction. *There's too much heart in me and none in you.*

When you decide to leave, leave me in the rain. For it knows how to calm every storm within me. *I won't feel alone, knowing the rain has always been my soulmate.*

It's an endangered species—people with a heart that not just beats but also feels. People who don't just understand poetry but let it cover every inch of their soul, the way monsoon clouds carpet the sky in late July.

Texting is easier because how do I look into your eyes and tell you that you're hurting me without crying? How do I look into your eyes and tell you I no longer see empathy in them?

You love cheesy fries, not regular ones. You love thin-crust pizza with a base not loaded with cheese but also not devoid of it. You only watch sunsets when you're sad because the pink hues remind you of everything you once used to be. You like rewatching your favourite movie and never take anybody's recommendations into consideration. You fold the sleeves of your shirt so casually, they're never the same length on both your arms. Your eyes widen when someone talks about your favourite band. You're uncomfortable in new restaurants, and there are only two restaurants that feel like home to you. You hate trying new places.

There's so much love in noticing what most people don't find worth noticing about someone—in being head over heels about the seemingly insignificant.

What we can't hold,
holds a special place
in our hearts.

It's the hands of someone
whose heart is the earth
and whose wavy hair is the ocean.
They carry all the love of the world
within them but none for you.

It's the lap of your grandmother
you can no longer sleep in
because she slept so peacefully,
it still breaks your heart.

It's your school
that shut down after you graduated.
By the time you heard the news,
they had already destroyed
your classroom.

What you can't hold
holds a special place
in your heart—
you have to love from a distance
but you hate the distance.

The way a kitten licks off the filth from its body to become clean—the licking is incessant, almost maddening. The same way I try to get rid of your scent from my skin.

When you write, the elite will hate you for it unless you're rich. They'll tell you that your words aren't worth reading because you're not friends with prominent people and studied in your own country. They'll tell you that your metaphors require complicated words, and that there must be something wrong in the kind of work that is so simple to understand. *They have a thing against writing that isn't pretentious because they cannot relate to it.*

If you're a writer, do not change your writing style because someone made you feel you're not worth it. Your poems can save lives. You're writing for people who think nobody understands them. You're writing for people who don't care about heavy words but only want their hearts to feel lighter. You're not a puppet of the privileged. Your words are fireflies that unknowingly pour light into hearts. *Nobody gets to define how your writing should read except your heart. Nobody.*

All my life, I was taught to have a plan—to know the next step, the step after that, and you guessed it right, the step after that. But I believe some dreams are achieved, some are forgotten, some you laugh at in the future and some don't remain your dreams anymore as you grow older.

I have a friend whose life choices made me unlearn this. She wanted to get married in her early twenties, and so she did. When her marriage turned toxic, she tried fixing things for a while, but when that didn't work out, she didn't put up with it and got a divorce. She wanted to be a teacher, so she became one. She spent over ten years teaching and realized she wasn't enjoying it anymore. Creative people cannot thrive in monotony. She quit her job and decided to open a cafe in the mountains with her boyfriend. She didn't want to rush into another marriage, so she didn't. She moved to the hills and started afresh. The cafe worked well for a few years, but then they had to shut it down. Was she upset that the cafe didn't work? Of course. Did that stop her from living her best life? Not at all. She moved out of the mountains, took up a job in another city and returned to teaching. Today, I received a message from her, telling me she'll be getting married to the guy she opened the cafe with.

I've known her for over eight years, and not once have I seen her not living her best life. She makes new friends, travels a lot, documents everything, hosts the best parties ever, and, most importantly, doesn't let anyone dictate how she should live her life. Nobody gets to decide when it's okay to change your mind and when it isn't. Nobody gets to stop you from changing career paths and cities. Nobody gets to tell you that your dreams are unrealistic. *To have no regrets is the ultimate dream, and that's the only 'plan' I care about.*

You're the kind of song one can't remember but knows they have listened to it before. The type of music that opens your heart and settles in the centre of your heart immediately. It's always within you, but you can't seem to remember the lyrics. Some people are like that—they cast a spell on you, and you don't even understand what made you fall for them this hard. *All you know is that you love them, and thanks to them, your body is no longer the home to your heart.*

A man with
a heart so pink,
that he spends
a lifetime
hiding it.

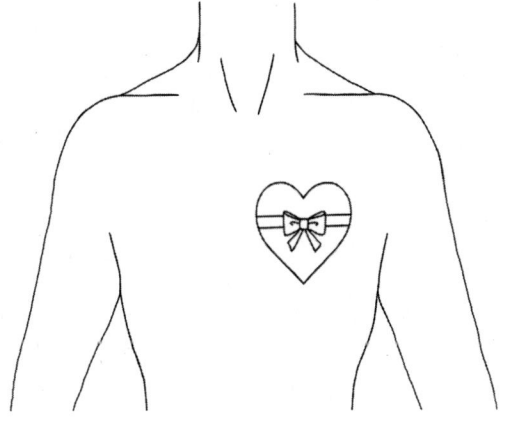

I heard the flowers cry
when you broke them
for someone who ended up
breaking your heart.

Why must you be a monsoon cloud in love?
Why must you destroy yourself to water the flowers in their chest?

When your best friend tells you that you deserve better, this is what they mean:

You're a product of Kintsugi.§ Your friends have seen you break a hundred times because there are more feelings in you than in a poetry book. They want you to fall in love with someone who wouldn't reopen the doors in your mind they've spent years trying to shut. They want you to fall in love with someone who wouldn't carry love in the back pocket of their jeans and anxiety in their arms. They don't hate the person you're dating because they want you to be single; they hate them because you always love with your whole heart, and not everyone understands how that works. Not everyone knows what it feels like to have someone who cares so much about them. Not everyone knows how to deal with a heart like yours. People have a tendency to break things they cannot handle, and your friends know how difficult it is for you to handle heartbreak. So, the next time your best friend tells you that you deserve better, I hope you know they're seeing what you don't. They are just trying to protect your heart.

§ The Japanese art of joining what's broken with gold.

Love is a bird
in a poet's house
and the world is full
of unsuccessful bird catchers.

Love doesn't want to fly;
it has never seen the sun,
the light will sting its eyes
because the world is meant
for more important things,
like power and pleasure.
So for love to survive,
it must hide itself
in the dark corners
of a poet's room
and not utter a word
lest it dies.

The only way of catching the bird called love is by catching hold of your own heart first. Stop trying to not feel things, okay?

The key to making everyone love you is unconditional tolerance, but the key to making sure everyone respects you is understanding that someone who consciously chooses not to treat you the right way doesn't deserve the right to stay in your life.

Remember when you were young and that relative told you that your crooked teeth required fixing? Remember how that statement stayed with you longer than you thought it would? Remember when you were friends with someone who constantly made you feel bad about yourself, and you never told them that it was hurting you because you wanted to be *nice?* Remember when someone disrespected your mother and you stood there in silence because you didn't want to call out someone older than you?

Everyone loves the kind of people who are unfamiliar with the concept of boundaries and self-respect. It is when they know they will have to watch their words and think twice before mistreating someone that they start feeling uncomfortable around them. *People lose interest in you when you start respecting yourself.* It's more convenient to be with someone you can hurt on a daily basis than to be with someone around whom you've to be mindful of your actions, knowing your words and actions have consequences.

Don't be the nicest person in the room—the one whose heart has been stepped on many times unregretfully—the one who would rather be unhappy than reprimand someone who is happy to see them in pain. Be the person who doesn't allow disrespect. Be the person who knows friendship and love don't come with sadism. *Be the person who knows how to treat people the right way, and more importantly, understands how important it is to be treated the right way.*

I wish God could immortalize flowers—
the ones in the gardens outside
and the ones in our hearts.

Our love is a wind chime that makes love to the wind to remind me that it's always there with me—within my reach, close to my heart.

You deserve someone who kisses you the way raindrops kiss flowers—gently and full of love. Have you noticed how the sky looks when it's drizzling—the sun shines softly, the clouds are still white and seem softer than the pillow you bury your head in at night. You deserve someone who makes you feel exactly like that moment. Someone whose love, like gentle raindrops, gives you the calm you deserve.

Whenever we fight, my abandonment issues convince me that you're about to leave me. And then the moon comes to life. And then I receive a text, '*Just because we're fighting doesn't mean I will go to sleep without saying goodnight. I love you.*'

I love you, you say. *I love you.* You don't tell me that you're leaving me. You don't ask me to apologize. You don't try to prove that I was wrong. You don't say anything my anxiety tells me you'll say, and you say everything my heart wants you to say.

'*I love you too,*' I respond and go to sleep, knowing there's so much love flowing within you, rivers would cry.

You always hug people as if it's the last time you're with them, and that's what happens when you feel too deeply—it suffocates everyone you love. Because people confuse your fear of losing them with obsession.

So many flowers are accidentally stepped on,
so many hearts are accidentally broken.

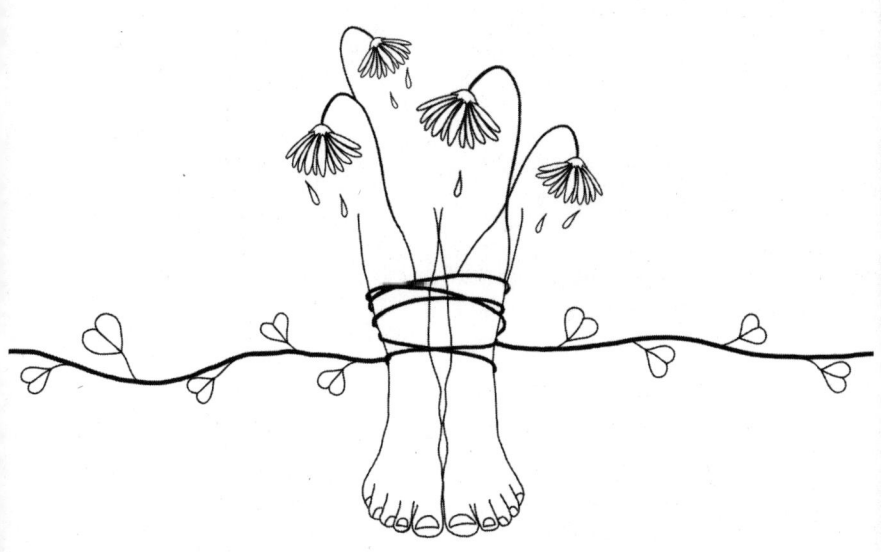

Some days,
when your mother will call,
you'll be too busy to pick up,
or you'll forget to call her back,
because there are too many things
on your mind that seem
far more important
than someone who loves you.

On those days,
she'll feed the sparrows
but the food will be wet
because of all the crying,
she never thought she'd be
jealous of birds eating together
until you left her alone.
She hasn't eaten properly
in a while.

Some days,
you'll forget to ask
your mother if she's okay,
and you wouldn't care
to make sure she's okay
on the days she tells you she isn't.

On those days,
she'll remember your smile
and go to bed a little early.
You'll sleep comfortably
unaware that she will be up all night.

Some days
you'll forget to
make your mother feel loved,
and her tragedy is that,
even on those days,
she'll love you.

You'll think that your world is synonymous with them—that if they left you, your entire world would collapse, too. But you're wrong.

One day, you'll wake up and notice a little boy plucking a small jasmine from the garden outside for the girl he likes, and it won't make your heart ache.

One day, a love song will play in a cafe and you'll catch yourself humming it. You won't feel the need to run out of the cafe and lock yourself in your room.

One day, you'll notice the way orange hues cover the sunset and take a picture of the sky because orange will no longer remind you of the shirt they wore on the first date.

One day, your heart will feel full and there'll be a smile stretched across your face like monsoon clouds in a July sky. You'll think that it's their memories that are making your heart so full, but then you'll try to think about them, and it'll take you a while to even remember their face.

One day, you'll be happy again, and I hope you remember that your world isn't going to collapse because someone left, and even if it did, you have what it takes to build it all over again.

Someone who allows their heart to feel fully can never be someone who forgets easily.

You still miss them because you never missed an opportunity to make them feel loved. You still feel homesick in their absence because you designated a permanent space for them in your heart. You still love them because they once made you feel loved. You can't get over them because there's more love inside you than stars in the sky.

Here we are, standing at the beach. You ask me to take a picture of you. I ask you to take off your glasses, and at that moment, I cannot help but notice how even the ocean looks shallow compared to your eyes. I swear, the moment you turned to the ocean, you stole its breath away too, for a while. I've never seen the ocean so still, almost as if all its waves were lost in your eyes.

When they ask you to *get over it,* I hope you remind yourself that healing isn't something someone gift-wraps and leaves at your doorstep. It's okay to feel like you won't get over it. It's okay to feel like you just *can't* get over it. Because 'it' once took up most of the space in your heart and nobody gets to decide when 'it' should stop mattering to you. Take your time, my love, and choose healing, no matter how slow it may seem to others. And I'm sorry if the people around you are being impatient with you. I'm sending love your way.

Do you like how they behave during arguments, or are you scared of that person?

Do they care to remind you that they still love you or let their anger take over to a point where you become your childhood self, hiding behind the door of your room and crying, because someone who claims to love you, forgets that you've feelings too during arguments?

If loving them feels like a war to you, remember that wars don't end in peace. Wars take away everything you love. They make you yearn for peace the way a stray dog yearns for stale chapatis people give it at the end of the day. *If it feels like a war, your victory lies in leaving them before the inevitable destruction unfolds.*

Disease kills the body, but loving the wrong person kills the soul. You wish to tame oceans for someone who won't mind leaving you alone.

You're trying to bury feelings
that are still alive.

Don't be surprised when
flowers blossom from them.

Sunsets carry the kind of sadness hearts are too weak to bear.

I sat alone in my room and counted the number of daggers on my back. I used to count the stars in the sky once. I prayed to God to help me find someone who will love me the way paper loves poems, prisoners love keys, parents love government jobs, artists love pain, clouds love shattering, flowers love rain, cats love their solitude and sleep, and pain loves the people who refuse to give up hope. I didn't believe in divine intervention until something divine made me meet you. I love counting the stars with you.

A list of reasons why I fell in love with you:

The last person you dated cheated on you. The last person I dated crushed my self-confidence like unexpected storms crush farmers' hopes. We were both too broken to break another person. We could trust each other because the people we loved had broken our trust.

After every fight, you choose me. You choose us. For the first time in my life, I see someone trying to stay with me. I have always been the one at war with myself because of others. This is the first time someone's willing to fight for me because they just love me so much.

When we were young and there was a fight at home, we would lock ourselves in a room. Some of us didn't even have the privilege of doing that. I remember calling you for comfort and crying. You told me that you were coming to pick me up. I didn't even have to tell you what was wrong.

You don't let me undervalue myself. '*I don't think this poem is good enough*,' I say, and you send me a list of reasons why it's the best poem in the world. I know I could write better than that, but you don't let me feel bad even for a second.

When we're watching a movie, you keep looking at me every once in a while, to check if I'm enjoying the movie too. You don't have to do it, but you do it anyway. It's been years since we've been together, and it still has remained the same.

We were supposed to go to a fancy restaurant on our first date. We were standing outside the restaurant and it began to rain. '*Do you want to take a walk in the rain?*' you had asked me, and that's when I knew I had found my soulmate.

There are more reasons to love you than raindrops in Mawsynram.⁵ I can write for an eternity but all it'll ever mean is that you're my soulmate. *You don't have my whole heart; you are my whole heart.*

---

⁵ The rainiest city in the world.

I didn't like myself before I met you, but I didn't hate myself either. It was only once you convinced me that I deserve to be loved, only to leave me for someone else eventually, that I understood how sometimes it takes another person for you to start hating yourself.

Does it qualify as healing if the only reason I think I'm okay without you is the fact that I don't get to see you anymore? Schrödinger's Cat theory** is true, the cat being my heart here. I don't know whether it will break all over again upon seeing you someday.

** A thought experiment that states that if you seal a cat in a box with something that can eventually kill it, you won't know if the cat is alive or dead until you open the box. So, until you open the box and observe the cat, the cat is simultaneously dead and alive.

I asked the flowers in my backyard how to get over someone. They flaunted the raindrops on their skin and said, '*Sometimes, you just can't do it.*'

Whenever it rains, the moment I feel the raindrops on my face, I wipe them off as quickly as possible. The moment I think of you, I distract myself immediately.

I want to prove them wrong—the flowers and my heart.

True happiness is in listening to the wind and birds sing in your absence, and realizing there's so much beauty beyond your face.

'*All successful people wake up early,*' they told me. Lately, I've realized that success is about having the privilege of sleeping like a baby all night and waking up a little late sometimes, just because it's raining and you feel like staying in bed a little longer.

The weather is perfect. The birds are singing more melodiously than usual. And you want to wake up and be productive because someone asked you to? Is being hard on yourself always a prerequisite for being successful?

They'll tell you that waking up at six in the morning will change your life, but they won't tell you that your life is yours to change—you get to decide how and when you need to work in order to change it for the better. It's okay if you're not a morning person.

You're a poem with missing stanzas and incomplete metaphors. Everyone you loved took parts of you that won't even fit anymore if you found them again. May you find someone whose love embellishes every metaphor in you, someone whose smile fills the void of every stanza you've ever lost.

I'm not someone who likes to fall asleep in someone's arms. I like my personal space. I like to sleep by myself. But then you came. They say you can hear violins when you're in love, but they're wrong. When you're in love, you hear your heart giggle for the first time. You discover music in your soul. You smile a lot more and don't want to be alone. Today, as you sleep beside me, I remind myself that nothing has changed, but then I look at my hands intertwined with yours. I realize I don't want to leave your hand. I admit I *like* my personal space, but I *love* you.

My back has more
daggers than skin.

Sometimes, I sit
with my silence
and think I am a bouquet
of fake flowers
on a dining table—
something that has
always ever looked
like it's blossoming;
something that has
always been dead.

One of the best feelings in the world is laughing your heart out with someone without worrying if they are going to eventually walk out of your life.

Yes, I'll make pancakes with you every Sunday morning. I'll show you every movie that turns my heart into a butterfly. I'll visit all my favourite places with you, knowing I won't ever have to visit them without a smile on my face—without you. I'll let you sleep in my arms when the cab ride is a little too long and without thinking twice, hold your hand in busy streets and dance in the rain with you when the rest of the world closes its windows and sleeps. *I'm convinced that once your heart knows someone's going to always stay with you, you love that person with your whole heart.*

When you got your first job, you wanted to buy concert tickets but ended up buying your sister a hardcover of her favourite book. The concert would end in two hours, but the book would end up making a permanent home on a shelf in your sister's heart. You bought a new wallet for your dad because you saw how the stitching of the old one had gotten damaged to the point that one day, the family photo fell off and he was upset the entire week. You bought tickets to a *kavi sammelan*[††] your mom really wanted to attend but couldn't the last time because she didn't want to spend money on herself. You took your best friend out for dinner and got to see it in her eyes that she was proud of you.

Don't get me wrong. It's not like you shouldn't want to do anything for yourself, but if you've been loved, your heart would want to do something for the ones who love you first. *It's just that you grow older and realize that you cannot be selfish because there are people who love you so selflessly that their happiness becomes more important than putting check marks on your bucket lists.*

You will get a job that pays well and go on that trip. You will buy clothes from that brand, party all night with friends, have overpriced pizzas that won't even taste nice and get those sunglasses without thinking twice—but you'll only feel like doing all of it after having done something for the ones you love. *And when you realize that the first person you want to buy something for with your hard-earned money isn't you, you know you're loved. You're privileged because this feeling isn't something everyone gets to feel.*

[††] Poetry meet.

You cross the airport and remind yourself that your grandmother is getting older and has never been on a flight. You study all night to get a scholarship so your parents won't have to pay the entire tuition fees. You don't think twice before asking your friends to split the bill because you don't want to put up an act your parents would have to pay for. You listen to your mom tell you the same story a thousand times. You sit with your family every evening to have chai together. It's been years since you stopped liking chai, but for you, it's a bonding exercise. You send books to your grandfather every month so that even on days you cannot go and remind him that he's loved, he still feels loved. You pretend to like your sister's boyfriend because he makes her happy. You don't make plans for New Year's because your mom likes it when the entire family begins the year together. That's how it works   we don't often ever say *I love you,* but we always feel loved.

You thought he was your soulmate—
someone who left your mouth
overflowing with unanswered prayers
and your heart, empty.

My soul is full of you,
the way oak trees are full of ants,
Mughal embroidery is full of floral motifs,
the flower girl's dupatta is full of mirror work
and her flowers are full of rain kisses,
the beggar's eyes are full of fading hope,
the sunset is full of stolen shades from flowers,
history books are full of lies,
monuments are full of names
engraved by couples who won't end up together,
sunflowers are full of the kind of darkness
they're too scared to face,
palaces are full of forgotten stories,
poets are full of grief,
poetry is full of hope,
empty homes are full of nostalgia,
busy streets are full of unfrequented bookshops.
My soul is full of you,
the way mornings are full of the sun—
your light reaches me every time.

A little boy who loves to paint measures weight for a living in a bustling Delhi bazaar. A little girl stands beside him and counts his bones. A few months ago, a privileged kid discarded some colours and a painting brush in a dustbin near where he sat. Today, when the little boy woke up, he realized someone had stolen his colours—the only thing that added colour to his life. His mother pulled him closer and said, '*The sunset stole the colours from your palette. Each day will end more beautifully now only because of you.*' She fed him a small paratha and went to sleep on an empty stomach. She didn't have the heart to tell him she had traded his happiness for his survival.

Every time you say goodbye,
you make me see
the butcher at the end of the street
with kinder eyes—
the way you shatter my heart
and leave it to bleed
and don't look back
to see the destruction,
not because you're too scared
of the aftermath
but because you've seen it
way too many times,
is something that could make
even the butcher break into tears.

You sometimes take a few
pieces of my heart with you
and I spend the rest of the day
trying to find them,
so I can put back together
what you broke.
I'm not unfamiliar
with the art of mending things
that shouldn't have been
broken in the first place,
but I don't know how not to break
knowing no matter how much I love,
I'm always the one who is left alone.

Have you seen how softly the sun shines at eight in the morning? As if it's here to warm not just your skin but also your heart. I'm convinced love should feel exactly like that. There should be gentleness so calming in love that your life becomes synonymous with the word peace. Love should come with the kind of softness that soothes your soul whenever life gets hard.

Growing up, I wasn't invited
to birthday parties or play dates.
So when a boy in the fifth grade
pity-invited me to his birthday,
I took out my favourite shirt,
asked my father to iron it,
kept looking at the clock
until it turned to six,
and rushed to the party
the way a dog rushes
to his owner when he returns from work.

For I yearned to feel belonged
more desperately than a child
who watches his mother fast every Thursday
and believes he can do it too,
only to watch his hunger take over him.
But the boy didn't acknowledge my presence—
I was a small birthday present
buried under all the huge ones,
not even a present, a surprise,
and not a pleasant one.

His friends didn't talk to me,
his parents asked why hadn't he
ever talked about me to them before,
everyone knew me, but they didn't want me there,
they saw me but pretended not to.
You see, there's this sadness in me,
that's palpable enough to drive you away
and scary for anyone who stays.

You don't make friends
with people with broken hearts
and smiles that have
only ever been met with frowns.
You don't make friends
with people who don't
have fun stories from family trips,
who sit in the classroom alone
because they don't want to be seen,
because they've never felt seen,
who stay quiet on most days
because silence is a way of postponing
violence at home,
who carry marks on their hands
that are not a result of juvenile pen fights in school,
who cry when nobody's watching
and sometimes in the middle of a crowd,
who are breaking when it's autumn outside
and continue to break even when spring arrives.
You don't make friends with people
whose insides are just as sad as their countenance outside,
whose hearts carry more rain than
a thousand monsoon clouds can contain.

Long story short,
growing up, I wasn't invited
to birthday parties or play dates,
so when a boy in fifth grade
pity-invited me to his birthday,
I made him a birthday card
and got him a friendship band—
he kept the card but declined the friendship.

So many of us feel like the novels that people don't choose to read because the cover isn't pretty enough.

It's been years since you left.

You once told me how you were not used
to waking up by yourself anymore.
The way my hand reached out
for the alarm clock in the morning
and my mind would wake me up
a few minutes before the first alarm,
so that it would be my voice that woke you up,
so that you wouldn't have to wake up to a blaring alarm
but to soft kisses that gave you more warmth
than your blanket ever could.

I wish I could tell you
that I still wake up before your first alarm,
and that all my mornings are empty without you.

People don't pick up poetry books because they fear they won't understand the poems. They might not be able to read between the lines. The metaphors might suffocate them and the imagery might be too confusing to comprehend. I think people do the same with people who feel too much. They choose to stay away from them because they fear they won't understand them. Their depths are too scary for them to delve into the beauty that lies within them.

When I first met you,
I saw a thousand poems
running towards me,
entering my chest
at a speed faster than light,
but still slower than the speed
at which I fell in love with you.

There are some songs you just cannot skip
—because they still remind you of someone
whose name once used to make your heart skip a beat.

It's raining. The car stops and I see paper boats drowning in a puddle outside. I look at the space between us and realize it's not just the paper boats that are drowning.

When someone asks me whom I have loved the most, I have an answer. Your name comes out of my mouth faster than little kids run to their mothers in crowded rooms. But when someone asks me who loves me the most, I don't have an answer. I look for you everywhere, but you don't even remember how I look. I love you in all languages, but you don't understand the language of my soul. I would bring the world to your feet, but you decided to leave me alone.

They ask me, 'Who has loved you the most?'
I tell them, 'Definitely not the person I love the most.'

The way your eyes turn into fairy lights on seeing their face. The way you miss them—like a bird misses her clipped wings. The way they feel like a gorgeous Sunday afternoon after a week full of dilemmas, deadlines and distress. The way they're the only book that isn't torn apart, smiling from the shelf of your life. The way they're everything you had heard about in moral science textbooks. The way they make your heart a flower dancing with the wind—deeply rooted in love but more liberated than ever.

You're a flower in a temple,
I, a flower on a grave.

You're made of all things happy,
I'm made of everything happiness
takes away with itself when it leaves.

I think flowers
have cursed us humans,
for they knew if we found
the kind of love they have—
the way the rain loves them,
the way the sun holds them,
the way the water wants them to grow—

if someone loved us enough
to never break our hearts too,
we'd bloom so bright
nobody would find flowers pretty anymore.

I found a place
to rest in your heart,
a place to hide my soul—
the only place
that made me feel seen,
the only person
who felt like home.

There's so much life within you that coexists with everyone who broke you. *Your heart is a graveyard full of rain.*

What will be left of this house when we abandon it? Will the walls tell the story of the violence to the people who live here next, or will the walls, among other things, be dismantled by the next family? Will the lilies in the backyard miss my mother's loving hands—the way she lovingly watered them every day, almost as if her life depended on it? Will the stairs remember how many times I almost tripped, but something saved me? Will the clock in the living room remember how our time in the house was always marked with dismay? *Will this house remember how home is a word we'll never be familiar with?*

Just because
I broke my heart for you
doesn't mean you're indebted
to break yours for me.

I don't love you the way
flowers love the rain
because it makes them grow.

I love you the way
the sun loves the earth,
my happiness lies solely
in pouring light into your soul,
and watching you bloom.

If you come closer to me, you'll find remnants of you in my eyelashes. I think this is why I don't wish upon fallen eyelashes anymore. My eyes always look tired because they're tired of waking up to your absence. They're darker than the rest of my face because I haven't slept peacefully since you left—the way a farmer cannot sleep knowing the flood took away everything he needed to stay alive.

In the heart of a person
who wears silence
like a prayer on his lips,
you will find a flowerless
plant called hope,
lying in the middle
of a thousand wildflowers
that are in full bloom,
even in the absence of the one
who planted them
but didn't love the person
enough to stay forever.

Drawing period in primary school. We were asked to paint our 'dream house'. My friends made houses that were so big that they looked like buildings. Some were creative enough to make igloos and houses by the lake. I, however, made a small house. From the window, you could see a family laughing together while having dinner. Years later, it is still my dream house.

Children are forbidden
from being children
by fathers who think
words like empathy and kindness
are reserved for their bosses,
in front of whom
they stand and accept ridicule
like kids accept candies on Halloween.

They come back home
and pluck dreams from the eyes
of their children the way
a florist plucks flowers in the morning.
The florist takes flowers everywhere—
to temples, graveyards and lovers,
but the father takes the flowers of dreams
and plucks one petal at a time,
almost like a *'he loves me, he loves me not'* game—
the mother knows he doesn't love his children.

They say that houses with children
are homes filled with laughter,
but what about houses that are turned into
architectures of grief
by someone who didn't process his own?

What about children who carry silence
like a birthmark they cannot get rid of?
They wear grief like a scent they were born with.
They can't help but smell of it all their lives.

What about mothers who have no choice
but to love their children more
than they have ever been loved?
She loves,
and loves,
and loves,
because she cannot leave.

There's so much about you that I'm yet to understand. So much of your heart I'm yet to see. I spend my days excited to learn further and I spend my nights trembling because uncertainty is a stepfather who doesn't believe in kindness on most days. I'm too in love with you to leave you, even after being acquainted with your ugliness.

When someone leaves,
their memories turn into a sparrow
that sits on the fence of your heart
when you least expect it.
You wait for it impatiently,
the way a patient's family waits
outside the ICU,
not knowing when
the operation will be completed.

There's a girl who felt
like jasmine flowers to me,
I miss her even on days
when all the flowers in the world
have stopped blooming.

When she left,
it was raining torrentially.
I didn't know
why torrential and torment
sound so similar
until she left me alone
in the rain.

There's an artist
who died on the street,
his paintings are drenched
in the rain,
the colours are now a mosaic,

a fading proof of something
beautiful that once existed.
We too are but a painting in the rain,
something beautiful that's now
drenched in pain.

I remember telling you how parallel lines break my heart because no matter how much they love each other, they can never be together. Today, as we sat together, you took my hand, placed it on your chest and told me, *this* is sadder. Being this close to someone and still not feeling anything at all. In fifth grade, when my math teacher taught us the concept of parallel lines, I remember getting scolded for joining the lines together. She then advised me to never merge things that aren't meant to be together. I understand now what she meant.

I see you with him,
holding his hand the way
paper boats hold the rain,
drowning in love with him
as I write this verse.

I see you with him,
laughing and giggling
like two little birds
who've just learned
how to fly.

Smiles so bright,
a love so full of light,
I wouldn't be surprised
if it brought
dead flowers back to life.

When it's 4 a.m.
and there are 40,000 thoughts
running in your head,
you stitch your scars with self-love
and call it healing.
When all you need
is one moment of relief,
when your sentiments
won't strangle your heart,
when your eyes
won't carry sad poems but glitter,
when your nose won't run
from all the crying,
when your heart won't run

towards someone who only
intends to add to your pain,
when you won't feel
this heavy all the time,
as if you had tragedies for breakfast
and fate was a locket tied
around your neck,
that now started feeling
like an albatross,‡‡
and you can feel yourself
suffocating just enough
to wish for death
but not enough to actually die.

I see you with him
And I remember you with me.
Ocean Vuong said,
'I miss you
more than I remember you,'§§
but to you I say,
I love you more than I miss you,
and I miss you more than you remember me.
You're the person who arose
hurricanes in my heart,
planted flowers in places
where only fear grew all this time,
turned my life into a vintage photograph
that looked like a dream

---

‡‡ A reference to the albatross in the poem 'The Rime of the Ancient Mariner' by Samuel Taylor Coleridge,

§§ *On Earth We're Briefly Gorgeous* by Ocean Vuong

to everyone who saw it,
not knowing that photographs are memories
and memories are proof of happiness,
but the present is proof of its expiration date.

I see you with him.
Anybody who writes about love
knows more about pain
than anybody else.
Anybody who knows about pain
knows pain is not something
people can give you,
it's something you give
yourself because of people.

I ask myself—what if you came back?
But then I wonder
if we were a poem God wrote
when she was too drunk,
if your metaphors found meaning
only when his eyes met yours.
And we were beautiful together too,
but we just didn't make sense.

If you come back,
I'll let you in
I'll show you how there's a graveyard now
where we had planted a garden together,
how memory is a toxic parent
who slaps you in the face twice a day
but hugs you once and you forgive it
for breaking your heart,

how lovers can forget everything but loving
and how loving seldom means
not breaking your own heart.

If you come back, I'll show you my heart.
There are memories stacked
like boxes of mangoes at the juice shop
we would frequent when were together.
If you come back,
I'll pack your memories in a box
and hand them over to you,
ask you not to build homes
out of people
when you've no intentions
of keeping them in your heart.

I sit next to my grandmother and struggle to continue the conversation in Hindi, my mother tongue. The colonizer's tongue is an oxymoron to me. It helps my words reach the world but is slowly taking me away from my world. My grandmother's hands trace my books as she tries to read the poems but in vain. My tragedy is that she could come across this page and still not know who it's about, so I'm leaving this word here—*naani*—so that she knows even in this book written in a language that's an ocean between her and me, there's still room for her. There always will be. This page belongs to the woman who may not understand what I write but who always understands my soul.

I wake up
to find the sun
kissing you before
I can hold you.

You make the sun
blush so much,
it looks a lot
like the moon.

'There are so many
pictures of me in your gallery.
I'm sorry for taking up so much space,'
she had once told me.
And I was worried she'd
faint if she ever saw my heart.

Dictionaries can give you definitions of words, but people get to define terms like 'love' and 'kindness' for you. For some, love has always been violence. For some, it's synonymous with absence. For some, it's the face of a person who had multiple opportunities to hurt them but chose not to. For some, it's a feeling they felt only briefly. My mother's presence is my closest acquaintance with kindness. My parents together are an oxymoron.

Yes, people will hurt you, and you will feel like removing them from your life—it's the first thought that will come to your mind, not because you're okay with losing them but because you're scared it'll happen eventually anyway. You think running away from someone will make your heart run out of pain. You assume that people are incapable of change and it's easier to live without them than with the fear of being hurt and broken the same way all over again.

But think about all the times they were the reason you didn't fall apart. All those days when they made you smile when nobody else could. All those memories that still make you feel lighter on days when life hurts a little too much. I don't want you to be someone who calls someone their best friend but lets go too easily. That's not how friendships work.

I don't want you to be someone who says '*I love you*' and changes it to '*I hate you. I can live without you. You never deserved me anyway*' over an argument. I know sometimes people hurt you so much that letting go isn't a choice anymore but the only option. Please don't break bonds the way you break flowers. There are voids that could've easily ceased to exist if you had just tried to fix things.

I choose you because, with you, my dreams aren't asked to exit. My opinions aren't asked to stay silent. My voice isn't made to stutter and my love isn't said to be too loud. My laughter is appreciated even in the most crowded settings. My hand is held in every busy street. I receive the longest hugs every time I leave. My cheeks are always wet with kisses and my heart is never devoid of love. With you, I'm loved for everything I've been hiding all my life. With you, loneliness is no longer my religion. And that doesn't make me an atheist because, with you, I believe in love. Only love.

People will step on your heart on purpose, write their name on your soul and then refuse to acknowledge that they ever knew you. They will promise to stay until the moon stops loving its silver shine and ask you to trust them, only to make you stop trusting people altogether. *The tragedy is that there are some people you continue to miss while dressing the wounds they caused. There are some people who own your heart in ways your self-respect doesn't.*

You yell at the top of your lungs that you will never forgive them, but your heart has already forgiven them. You were never even angry at them for hurting you because you were just scared that the fight would turn into a break-up. You say you're okay with letting them go for the sake of your well-being, but this very thought turns your heart into a child sitting alone in his room at night as the light goes off. You're terrified of losing them even though you know all they've ever done is cause you pain.

Have you ever felt physically incapable of being mean to someone? You're in an argument with someone you love dearly, and the person ends up saying the worst things to you, but your reaction isn't even half as brutal as theirs. You know you can hurt them as well, but a fist-sized rebel in your chest tells you not to. You would rather break into tears than break their heart. You know if this argument took place between you and someone else, you wouldn't let go so quickly. You wouldn't stay quiet. You wouldn't break into tears.

You deserve someone who feels this way when you're in the middle of a fight. Someone who chooses not to hurt you and who you choose not to be mean to either. When you're in love with someone, you know you can hurt them easily because you know things about them that stay hidden from the rest of the world. But I think there's so much love in choosing not to hurt the other person, in choosing not to use someone's insecurities only to win a petty fight, and in choosing to be kind when it's difficult. You don't deserve someone who apologizes after saying hurtful things to you. You deserve someone who consciously chooses not to cross boundaries because they believe every argument, every fight, every mismatch of opinions is less important than you at the end of the day.

My best friend says
I'm always rushing
to replace broken things
so I don't have
to look at them anymore.

When the clock broke,
I immediately went out
to buy another one.
When my favourite chair broke,
I rushed to the market.
I think I can get over things
faster if I replace them
with something else.

But when I broke,
I was left with
nowhere to go.
I realized there isn't
another me to replace me,
there are no mirrors in my room,
I can't afford to look
at something so broken,
something so irreplaceable
every day.

You don't deserve to wake up with a pain in your chest that has nothing to do with physical health and everything to do with the way someone's hurting you repeatedly. You don't deserve to spend your days trying to control your tears—in metro rides back home, when you're eating out with your friends, when a familiar song plays at a cafe, when you're by yourself in your room—only because someone refuses to be gentle with your heart. You don't deserve to have meltdowns in the middle of office meetings, cry while changing gears of your car, shut your windows to block all the light in the world and blame yourself for what an inconsiderate, horrible person did to you. *Second chances aren't a bad idea, but some people are just bad people, and no matter how much you break yourself for them, they're going to make you feel bad about yourself—they will break your heart all over again.*

Five years ago, when I fell in love, I hoped the person would stay with me forever. In love, we shouldn't turn into butterflies, I would say. Love can't be fleeting—the way butterflies love a different flower every day. In love, we should be the ocean—consumed by something beyond beautiful. Stronger together, unchanged, unbothered and unaffected by anything that comes our way.

Today, I'm a different person. I know forever is too much to promise. I know people fall out of love. I know people end up falling in love with other people. And I know my soulmate will simply stay, without me having to ask for a promise of forever. I'm learning to be okay with watching people leave. I'm learning to accept that there are some people who just date you; they never fall in love with you, and that's okay.

Even forest fires are scared of your softness.

170

Why must you wish
to be a rose
that's loved only
when it's blooming,
or a sunflower
that needs someone's
light to feed on?

If you wish
to be a flower,
be the kind they don't
put in bouquets
and lovers don't pluck
for each other.

Be the kind of flower that
doesn't need someone
to call her beautiful,
the kind of flower
that doesn't feel left out
because someone
didn't choose her.

The kind of flower
that keeps blooming
because that's what
she was made for—
being happy by herself
without wondering why
someone didn't find her
pretty enough.

171

You can't love hard if the softness in your heart isn't consistent. It can't rain every other day while the other person is left wondering if a rainbow will even show up. If you can't promise them gentleness, don't build a home in their heart.

After a fight, it's strange how sometimes giving them space suffocates you.

Silence is a storm if you are scared of solitude.

I hope your heart
runs into someone
whose love ends up
running through your veins.

My father gifted my mother silence,
but her struggles gifted her a voice.

I wonder what I've inherited,
for I struggle to voice
how I feel when I'm struggling.

I'm convinced
there are poems
stitched within your silence,
and only I should be allowed
to listen to them.

We've been convinced we must first be drenched in the storm to experience the rainbow. We need to study eighteen hours a day to build a career. A scientist must never take a break if they want to make a breakthrough. A writer must never take a break if he wants his next book to be a bestseller. A corporate employee must never take a break if he wants to be promoted. We must suffer before we watch the rainbow. We must spend a whole lot of time in pain to experience even an ounce of happiness. Why must it be like that? I want to work, but I don't want to only work. I want to build a career but not at the expense of friendship and love. I want to get a promotion, but I don't want to skip meeting my mom over the weekend because working a little more would bring me closer to a potential promotion. I want to work, but I don't want to be stuck in a toxic environment. The rainbow will surely be worth it, but I don't want my existence to be marked by endless storms for me to finally be able to watch it.

Sometimes, when you want someone to build a home in your heart, you forget that you're used to the existing architecture of your heart. There are memories tucked in every corner. Some walls are painted in the colours that someone left behind. There are leftovers of everyone you've met in life. Letting someone build a home inside you also means letting them repaint your heart. You're allowing them to take over something that has always been taken for granted. It's okay to be scared. I hope they end up staying always.

Have you seen how suddenly it starts raining sometimes? One moment, the sun is shining bright, and the next, you're entirely drenched. Pain and rain have so much in common.

Some people will tell you that you miss the feeling, not the person, but I don't think that's true because I'm certain it's you that I miss. It's your jet-black hair and your smile that resembled the kind you see in paintings of princesses from medieval India. It's the way your hands felt intertwined with mine. It's the way we'd sit together comfortably in silence and do nothing. It's the way I didn't have many thoughts around you, but I knew I was happy. I don't miss the feeling; I miss you, but perhaps you were a feeling too.

Is there someone whose name is an embellishment you wear on your soul?

You don't consider them an umbrella to protect yourself when it rains; you wish to protect them from every storm in the world. Someone who carries a longing for you in their eyes even when you've made it clear that it's them you belong to. Someone who loves you so much that it makes you feel like all your dreams have been personified and taken the shape of their face, with eyes that promise you that they'll stay forever and a heart that reminds you they don't make promises to break them.

Girls like you deserve flowers so heavenly that their scent stays with you all day, like a warm embrace. Picnic dates where conversations are so romantic, you feel like you're living in a novel. Heartfelt notes left on refrigerators, front seats at concerts, books that feel like home, friends who make you laugh till your cheeks hurt, lovers who write poems for you and monsoon afternoons spent dancing in the rain. Girls like you deserve someone who doesn't just get you flowers but brings the spring to your soul. Don't settle for anything less.

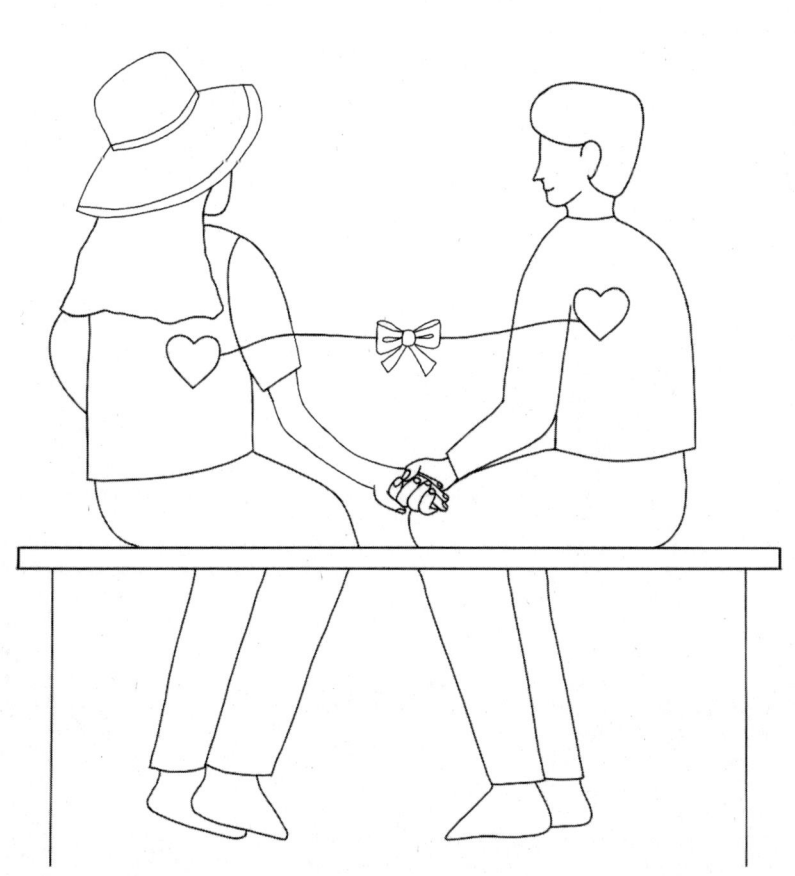

Boys like you deserve sloppy kisses and hugs so warm that the world feels jealous. Someone who writes letters for you on days when you're not okay and gives you reassurance without you ever having to ask. To discover new pizza places where everything tastes too heavenly to even describe. To dance to your favourite songs at midnight with your favourite people. Friends who are happy to see you smile. Lovers who never let you feel alone. Pancakes, cherry blossoms and custom playlists. You deserve someone who loves you so much that even on your saddest days, you still remember that joy exists when you look into their eyes and watch love overflowing. Don't settle for anything less.

Perhaps you are not letting
them go because you would
rather be stuck in storms with
them all your life than be in
silence by yourself even for a
while. You are not as much in
love with them as you are
scared of being alone. I hope
you summon enough courage to
ask them to leave, and when
they do, I hope you tell them—
thank you for leaving.

If you enjoyed reading this book, please write to Rithvik at @wordsofrithvik on Instagram. He'd love to hear from you!

Scan QR code to access the
Penguin Random House India website